BRIEF OVERVIEW OF DIALOGICAL PSYCHOTHERAPY

Tim Kellebrew

TiLu Press LLC

TiLu Press, LLC
11918 SE Division Street NUM 178
Portland, OR 97266 USA

This is a TiLu Book.

Note: The First Edition of Brief Overview of Dialogical Psychotherapy was published in 2012 by TiLu Press. This Revised Second Edition (2020) replaces that edition. Both editions are based in part upon a paper that was published in 2006 in a UK philosophy journal under the title of: Dialogical Self, Dialogical Other: A Brief Overview of Dialogical Psychotherapy, by Tim L. Kellebrew. Both editions of this work include updated content that is quite different from that original paper.

ISBN-13: 979-8566721125

Cover design by: Li Jili

Printed in the United States of America

CONTENTS

PROLOGUE

The philosophy of Martin Buber as a philosopher of dialogue is well known to philosophy, philosophy of religion, and philosophical anthropology. His thoughts and how they have been applied to counseling and psychotherapy are however, less well known. This brief work presents an overview of some of the modern and postmodern therapists and analysts who have drawn from Buber's philosophy important principles that guide their clinical practice. Drawing upon the distinction made by Maurice Friedman (2003) between *therapists of dialogue* and *dialogical therapists*, the basic elements of a dialogical approach to counseling and psychotherapy are discussed. Some of the philosophical implications of the development of self and other in the therapeutic context are also briefly mentioned.

SECTION I. INTRODUCTORY THOUGHTS (HISTORY AND DEVELOPMENT OF A DIALOGICAL PSYCHOTHER- APY).

In counseling and psychotherapy, there have been a number of therapy approaches based upon the idea of dialogue with both children and adults. Some of these approaches have explored the possibilities of a Dialogical Self, have drawn from the works of Bakhtin (1986) and others from the Soviet school, or emphasized the work of Hermans (2002). (Some definitions of a Dialogical Self include constructs associated with multiple voices within an individual. The person must then make a narrative, guiding them through situations). Another approach from Finland is Dialogical Sequence Analysis which is being used in what some have called a Dialogical approach to counseling or psychotherapy that utilizes the work of Mikael Leiman (2004). Some have also termed this approach Cognitive Analytic Therapy (or CAT.)

Instead of focusing on the approaches that emphasize a Dialogical Self, this book draws upon the work of a philosopher who has not yet received widespread attention for his ideas applied to counseling or psychotherapy: Martin Buber and his notions of a philosophical anthropology, the importance of dialogue, (also known as his philosophy of dialogue) and healing through meeting. These ideas and others have led to a *Dialogical Psychotherapy* developed by Buber and his followers. This book describes *this* Dialogical Psychotherapy as it has unfolded, discussing its implications for the practice of counseling and psychotherapy.

My discussion will also show how the two views of Dialogical Self and Dialogical Other differ. As one approach appears to be more constructivist in terms of the individual's thinking or emotional process and the other appears to focus more on the interpersonal realm. Although, both the Dialogical

Self and Dialogical Other approaches do address the constructs of self and other in each view, Dialogical Psychotherapists from Buber's perspective have not traditionally thought of intrapsychic thinking and processes as dialogue, but rather as instances of dialectic and monologue (Friedman, 1989). Neither can the dialogical be reduced to mere speech acts, although speaking certainly is often a part of the therapy process. This is not to belittle their importance.

Many therapists place great value on both domains of work, such as the dialectical or the dialogical in therapy and counseling work. Let us define from the Buberian perspective, what we mean: in the dialogical we are speaking about the intentionality of two persons relating to each other in a special kind of relationship, and in the dialectical, we have the concept of the opposition between two points of view (Hycner, 1991).

Ultimately, when one considers the distinction of dialogue and dialectic-said distinction blurs when considering personal development throughout one's course of therapy or developmental lifespan. Whereas dialectic and dialogue could represent different phases of development in life and therapy, they may very well be important phases for key historical moments that interplay as a unity of personal and social direction. Thus, the realms of the dialectical and dialogical can be quite complementary. And working in both realms is quite beneficial to many of our patients. However, in Dialogical based work, therapists pay special attention to approaching the patient as a person to person. Not to say that dialectical work obscures the person of course, but dialectical work can be done without another person being present, and dialogical work requires another person.

Although therapists might argue in the purest sense that dialectic and dialogue are two separate aspects of doing therapy work, this view may limit the possibility of moving back and forth between the two realms as readily as one might. The two realms may have as much interplay (dynamic interaction) as the philosophical concepts of subject-object deliberation (Kellebrew, 1984) or the interplay of the two primary spheres of relation, such as I-It and I-Thou (Buber, 1958).

There are other therapies that may blur this distinction at times, and some therapies that start from a foundation of dialectics. This is illustrated by the schools of thought or therapies based on dialectical thinking (Basseches, 1984) and the Dialectical Behavior Therapy (DBT) of Marsha Linehan (1993).

To those practitioners who wish to base their approach upon more of a Buberian perspective (or to add dialogical elements to a dialectical therapy they practice, this book can be especially helpful). One may find even more tools in their toolbox! Since dialogue occurs only between two persons in the between, or interhuman realm of meeting where genuine dialogue occurs, there is no pretense (honesty is also important in DBT!), leading us to a place where moments of significant meeting may occur. In my opinion, moments of dialectic and dialectical based training may make one even more responsive to the dialogical realm of therapy work. One returns to the dialectical realm after dialogue, works there through accommodation, and comes back to dialogue based on what they now know. (This last sentence implies that the two procedures are less reciprocal than they really are).

In review, the two distinct concepts of Dialogical Self and Dialogical Other may represent different operational meanings of the term *Dialogical*. (However, dialogical therapists would likely state that the term *dialogical* is restricted to the sphere of what they call *the between*). Alternatively, adherents to the Dialogical Self notion might state that another person's voice may become part of a solitary person's inner work and that this work is still dialogical (Smythe, 2013, Hermans, 2002). While dialogical therapists on the Buberian side of things would insist that reflection without the immediacy of the other person remains dialectical and Is not dialogical at all. Such dialogical therapists would insist upon the encounter between person and person as the dialogical relation. (The reasons for this, will I hope, become apparent as one reads on in this book).

In this view, dialogical therapists may not readily accept intrapsychic notions as being dialogical, as dialogue requires two persons and a way of being with another person. Whereas dialectic and dialogue may be viewed as important joint aspects of any single therapy that moves toward healing through meeting (Trüb, 1952; Hycner, 1993; Buber, 1952). *Healing through meeting* is a central focus of dialogical work, as it is understood and practiced by dialogical therapists. (I will discuss a full definition of *healing through meeting* in a later section of this book).

My discussion in Section II begins with defining some of the key concepts of Buber's work that have influenced Dialogical Psychotherapy. For now, I shall mention some of the works and ideas that are foundational and historical to such a Buberian based Dialogical Psychotherapy. Obviously, we shall begin with Buber. Although many of Buber's works and lived out relationships with others formed the basis of Dialogical Psychotherapy, the major works I draw upon are *I and Thou* (Buber, 1958, originally published 1923); *The Knowledge of Man* (Buber, 1965a); and *Between Man and Man* (Buber, 1965b); as well as Buber's Foreword to Hans Trüb's (1952) work, *Heilung aus der Beregnung* (Reprinted in Buber, 1952). (Which is roughly translated as *Healing Through Meeting*). These works are indispensable to understanding the philosophy of the dialogical approach that comprises Dialogical

Psychotherapy.

After the rightful mention of Buber as foundational and inclusive to any solid Dialogical Psychotherapy, I shall then turn to a discussion to the works of those who have carried it further. Friedman (1985, 2003), Hycner (1991; 1993), and Heard (1993), arguably offer us the most important works on Dialogical Psychotherapy as a distinct approach to psychotherapy and counseling to date. Finally, I shall turn to a brief discussion of Hans Trüb, who, predating many of the above therapists, led the way to a true Dialogical Psychotherapy.

Also, as Mouladoudis (2001) and Friedman (1985; 2003) have both stated, a number of therapists have drawn upon the work of Martin Buber to inform their clinical practice. However, there is a large difference between *therapists of dialogue* and *dialogical therapists* (Friedman (2003); italics mine). Upon making this important distinction, Friedman (2003) points out that dialogical therapists have made healing through meeting central to their approach to the client and draw directly upon Buber to guide their clinical practice. Friedman (2003) then mentions the following therapists as examples of dialogical therapists: Hans Trüb, Leslie Farber, Richard Hycner, and William G. Heard (among others). After looking briefly at historical antecedents to a Dialogical Psychotherapy, including Friedman's own work, I shall return to a more detailed discussion of several of these dialogical therapists in Sections III and IV of this work.

Regarding the work of Maurice Friedman, it is in his work that we have some of the first organized efforts in terms of Dialogical Psychotherapy. For as early as the third revised edition of his *Martin Buber: The Life of Dialogue,* Friedman (1976) includes a chapter on psychotherapy, where he mentions both the work of Hans Trüb and Viktor Von Weizsäcker as early examples of dialogically oriented therapists. Friedman (1975) also wrote an early article that spoke of a dialogical approach to psychotherapy, and it is in his important book, *The Healing Dialogue in Psychotherapy* (1985) that we have the first important text in the practice of Dialogical Psychotherapy.

Mouladoudis (2001) in his comparison of the Dialogical Psychotherapy approach with Carl Rogers' Person Centered Approach, mentions the same important connection between Maurice Friedman and Dialogical Psychotherapy, and it is Maurice Friedman, as a major interpreter of Buber's work for many decades, that has proven foundational to the other thinkers and dialogical therapists just mentioned. (This is not, however, to say that Dialogical Psychotherapy did not have other historical antecedents (most notably, the work of Hans Trüb). Later, regarding usage of the exact terms, Hycner (1993) states that the actual name *Dialogical Psychotherapy* as a distinct approach of therapy, was first used in 1983 or 1984 (at the Institute of Dialogical Psychotherapy-an institute that was co-founded by Hycner himself, James DeLeo, and Maurice Friedman).

Early antecedents to a dialogical psychotherapy are present in Buber's own work. In 1957, Buber was invited to the United States to give a series of lectures at an institute of psychiatry. Buber conducted seven seminars, three of which were on his understanding of the unconscious (Friedman, 1965). Some of these were later published as essays in *The Knowledge of Man* (Buber, 1965a) and in Buber (1999). Also in 1957, it should not be overlooked that there are aspects of Buber's ideas applicable to Dialogical Psychotherapy that can be drawn from the interesting dialogue that he had with Carl Rogers on April 18, 1957 (Buber, 1965a). Buber's introduction to Trüb's reprinted book, *Heilung aus der Beregnung* (Trüb, 1952) has also been reprinted (after translation to English) in *Pointing the Way* (Buber, 1952). Said introduction (Buber, 1952), contains many comments about psychotherapy from a dialogical perspective. Finally, it is the work of Trüb itself (Hycner, 1993) that describes other important antecedents to Dialogical Psychotherapy.

SECTION II. MARTIN BUBER'S PHILOSOPHICAL ANTHROPOLOGY: FOUNDATIONS OF A DIALOGICAL PSYCHOTHERAPY.

Martin Buber, the Austrian born Jewish philosopher, thinker, and philosophical anthropologist is perhaps best known for his work on the spheres of relation termed the I-Thou and the I-It. As Friedman (1965) and many others have pointed out, a philosophical anthropology begins with the problem of the human, what makes one human, how does one stand in relation over against one another, and to what extent do we have to do with one another. In psychotherapy, as in other realms of human living there is no I without the Thou, but in therapy it is the address of the world that the client must also address in his response to the authentic dialogue between them and that of the therapist.

I-Thou and I-It

These two types of relation were first mentioned and described in Buber's 1923 original work, *I and Thou* (Buber, 1958). Friedman (1986) describes both as modes of human existence that oppose and complement one another. We would not exist without them. In the world of I-It, we have the subject-object relation, the relation of persons to things as objects, and to other persons as objects. In the world of I-Thou we have the graceful appearing of a person one over against another, encountering one another in a special manifestation of meeting in the interhuman (also known as *the between*). In I-Thou we have the encounter between a person and person, but not every encounter is an instance of I-Thou. It is expected that both I-Thou and I-It will be aspects of human experience, with there being many more occasions of I-It than purely I-Thou.

The Interhuman, also Known as The Between

The interhuman, or *between,* is an ontological domain of relating that is more than the additive aspects of two persons that happen to one another, or even their joint totality; it is the essence of what happens between them. Buber (1965a) described aspects of the interhuman, among which are that humans agree to be authentic to one another in their communications. Buber says when this becomes mutual, we have genuine dialogue. This dialogue is a ground for being instead of seeming in our approach to an other, when we turn to an other in all truth. Finally, Buber describes another element that represents a choice point that humans must make in their encounters with others in the between, and that is the question of imposition or unfolding. Are we going to help the other person unfold or impose a view upon them? The preferred answer is obvious in a Dialogical Psychotherapy. Although both imposition and unfolding point to the ontological significance of the between, according to Buber (1965a), it is the process of unfolding that uncovers potential.

It is here between person and person that we have the cardinal manifestation of any proposed Dialogical Psychotherapy, that is, the meeting of a person with another person in the between. Where other therapies may speak more of an intrapsychic connection, with the client doing the work inside themselves, perhaps guided by a therapist or counselor, in Dialogical Psychotherapy the world of individual psychology (termed *psychologism*) is merely the accompaniment of the dialogue that must occur for meeting to take place. In a sense then, there is no such thing as a truly Dialogical Self from the Buberian perspective; instead, it is the relationship itself and the dialogue that goes with it that underscores change in the client or patient. (Friedman and other dialogical therapists such as Hycner have defined intrapsychic moments of self-knowledge as moments of monologue or dialectic, something that Trüb also commented on). In a dialogical therapy then, the person happens to the other person and reality unfolds in the interhuman realm between them, and it is there, in that relationship, that healing through meeting occurs.

This is not to say that the between is as simple as moving from the realm of the intrapsychic to the realm of the interpersonal, rather it is something qualitatively different from both aspects. Unmistakably, the realm of the interhuman is not synonymous with the realm of the interpersonal, rather, it is the particularized concreteness made manifest by an appearing at a unique time when I encounter a client; a time that if our dialogue is based on authenticity we may encounter an I-Thou moment between us. Yes, in Dialogical Psychotherapy, it is a time to respect the client's story, but it may equally be a time to oppose them in a tension to help them become who they were called to become.

This realm of the *interhuman* does not make Dialogical Psychotherapy indefinable, it merely points to the dialogical dynamics inherent in it. One takes the approach of genuine dialogue, and the deliberate stance of those who go out to meet an other, keeping one foot in their own worlds and one foot in the client's while never losing sight of their own. This uniqueness, this encounter, that you have in a historical moment with your client is in the moment that presents the between to you and them and grants to you both the opportunity of an appearance of I and Thou.

The true dialogical therapist is informed and merely guided by Buber's ideas, but their application is what happens in the lived-out encounter between the therapist and the client. It is not the techniques that get lived out, because there are no techniques per se, it is the dialogue and the meeting, because all real living is meeting (Buber, 1958). This leads us to the true domain of a Dialogical Psychotherapy as a consideration of the living experience of what happens in the between. The dialogue and the relation is what is important. In every sense of the word, in a dialogical moment one happens to another. Despite this *presentness*, that is, *making the other present*, there is a dialogical stance that can be taken by the therapist, and it is this stance that is informed by what others have already discovered in the dialogical approach.

Dialogue in Distance and Relation

Approaching a client in terms of Dialogical Psychotherapy means that there must be a willingness to approach the other (in this case a client), to accept them, to confirm them for who they are and, ultimately, who they are called to become. (As Buber, (1965a), told Carl Rogers, there is a difference between acceptance and confirmation, as confirmation implies endorsing their potential). One approaches within genuine dialogue, but one cannot expect a full mutuality in this type of dialogical relating, but through the act of *inclusion* (which is not the same as empathy) there is a bold swinging of the therapist into the life of the other to relate to her, to have genuine dialogue with her, and it is only then that those who suffer the most from the most grievous of psychological maladies can be aided in their existential state of affairs that has been arrived upon from an atrophied personal center. (This is a limited mutual act of inclusion because the client cannot be expected to have the same mutuality for the therapist, and as such it represents the second of three types of dialogical relating which has to do with inclusion that Buber has described (1965b)).

In distance and relation, we have another aspect of Buber's philosophy of dialogue. If, according to Friedman, (1965) understanding the elements of the interhuman (or the between) is more of an application of Buber's philosophy of dialogue and distance and relation is more developmental-then we have a philosophy that originates relation, establishes initial relation, and causes it to blossom if general conditions and particulars are met. In distance and relation, we have two movements, the first Buber called: "the primal setting at a distance," the second movement Buber termed: "entering into relation," (Friedman, 1965, p. 21). If one is not able to set another at a distance, then one is not able to enter into a relation with them, as distance is the presupposition, it is the only way we can approach and ultimately enter relation. Entering relation is the only way by which we become more whole, that is, we become an I only with a Thou, (and this is the opposite of any self-psychology). Finally, "the goal is completing distance by relation, and relation here means mutual confirmation, co-operation, and genuine dialogue," (Friedman, 1965, p. 21). In Dialogical Psychotherapy, one understands these two movements; that both are necessary, but we often don't understand it when the client displays them in the therapy!

Meeting and Mismeeting

Although it is impossible in such a brief work to list all the aspects of Buber's philosophy of dialogue that could be applicable to psychotherapy, I cannot leave out the general principle of meeting and mismeeting. For it is in the realm of meeting where healing takes place. Everything about Buber's philosophy prepares one to adopt the deliberate stance of preparation for meeting. When you encounter a patient, it becomes your responsibility to do all that you can to arrange an opportunity for a true meeting to take place between you both.

As Buber (1958), has said: "all real living is meeting" (p.11). A meeting is a special event that can happen when two persons encounter each other in genuine dialogue. (A mismeeting occurs when they fail despite attempts to do so, have an actual proximal encounter without really connecting, or have a deep and shocking misunderstanding). A meeting is not necessarily a willed event; it is the type of dialogue that one leaves sensing that something significant has just happened. At other times it may simply be that no opportunity for dialogue occurred despite the wish from someone that it would have. We will have these events throughout our lifetimes at key points, and just as significantly, we will have the hurts of *mismeetings* also. Buber used special words to describe what these are like. The concept of meeting was born out of his own painful encounter with *mismeeting* as a child. It is recounted by biographers (Friedman, 1981), representing a key moment when Buber was talking with his older sister, he realized that his mother had abandoned them at his grandparents, and would never return.

Not only will these types of human experiences and events take place throughout a person's lifetime, they can also occur in therapy. Obviously, the idea is to try to avoid a mismeeting with a client, but sometimes unforeseen events occur if a client feels they have been misunderstood by the therapist, the therapist has not approached them in accordance with dialogical principles, or there is some injury in the between perpetuated, even accidentally, inadvertently or, worse yet, on purpose by the therapist. If possible, mismeetings should be remedied by the act of reparation through further dialogue, as that is the recommended and the re-sponsible course of action.

SECTION III. BASIC ELEMENTS OF A DIALOGICAL PSYCHOTHERAPY

As stated above, a Dialogical Psychotherapy has as its core the philosophy of Martin Buber. In addition to an understanding of Buber's philosophical anthropology, there is also an engagement in the life of dialogue itself. For, if dialogue and meeting take place in the sphere of the *between* or interhuman, then a Dialogical Psychotherapy takes place there also. In short, in Dialogical Psychotherapy we have a counseling and therapy approach that is all about the relationship in the between and what happens in it. As Maurice Friedman has defined it: "By dialogical psychotherapy we mean a therapy that is centered on the meeting between the therapist and his or her client or family as the central healing mode, whatever analysis, role playing, or other therapeutic techniques or activities may also enter in," (1992, p. 52; 2003, p. 55).

According to Rich Hycner (1991) a Dialogical Psychotherapy means that its overall approach, process, and goal is grounded in the dialogical. Hycner defines the term *dialogical* as not referring to speech, as such, "...but rather to the fact that at its most fundamental level human existence is inherently relational," (1991; p. 4). Hycner goes on to state that it is there in a relational realm where dialogue takes place, a place where the self and the systems approach appear both jointly and in transcendence of one another at the same time, it is there where one enters the realm of the *interhuman* (1991, pp. 4-5). It is there where Dialogical Psychotherapy takes place.

In my overview of Dialogical Psychotherapy, I shall examine the works of several of these dialogical therapists and the elements they mention as defining aspects of the therapy. Because this book is an overview, interested readers are encouraged to explore the works of these therapists directly (as listed in the Bibliography), as well as the cogent and thorough paper on this subject drafted by Maurice Friedman (2003). I shall now turn to a few of the ideas presented by the following therapists: Maurice Friedman, Richard Hycner, William Heard, and Hans Trüb. For in addition to the foundation of Martin Buber's ideas, we have particularly evident in these dialogical therapists, many additional ideas that help us to develop an understanding of the practice of Dialogical Psychotherapy.

Maurice Friedman

In his important work on Dialogical Psychotherapy, Friedman sets out the basic elements of the Dialogical Psychotherapy approach (Friedman, 1985) and shows how healing through meeting has informed much of psychology and psychotherapy already. He defines other core factors that work through confirmation and healing through dialogue. Such factors include the important work of confirmation, the unconscious, dreams, inclusion, and Friedman's own contribution to Dialogical Psychotherapy, the *Dialogue of Touchstones*. Friedman has revisited these core factors, adding other elements of a Dialogical Psychotherapy in his discussion already cited (Friedman, 2003). However, it was in the 2003 article that he more explicitly and more elaborately outlined these and other factors of a Dialogical Psychotherapy in discussing the following ten elements:

1) The Between or Interhuman;

2) Recognition of the Dialogical;

3) Underlying the Two Movements of I-Thou and I-It (As an Element of Distance and Relation);

4) Healing through Meeting;

5) The Unconscious seen as Buber saw it;

6) Existential Guilt;

7) Inclusion, or *Imagining the Real*;

8) The Problematic of Mutuality;

9) Confirmation; and,

10) The Dialogue of Touchstones; (Friedman, 2003, pp. 56-65).

I shall now briefly look at these elements, giving a simple definition of each. Some of these elements are also discussed in other sections of this book, but in those cases my discussion is contextually different and aims to cover the element in such a way as to further the reader's understanding of the element as it would be applied to a Dialogical Psychotherapy.

Element 1: The between or inter-human

Already briefly discussed in Section II on the philosophy of Buber. This is a special dimension of ontological significance between person and person that is often overlooked because of the way we divide the world into inner and outer, subject and object (Friedman, 2003, pp.56-57).

Element 2: Recognition of the Dia-logical

This is the understanding that the psychological is only an accompaniment to dialogue, that meeting is the essential element of human existence, and that we relate to others not just from our own experience but from their uniqueness and otherness (Friedman, 2003, p.57).

Element 3: Underlying the two Movements of I-Thou and I-It is a Twofold Element of Distance and Relation

As already discussed in Section II, Friedman has stated that Buber saw this as absolutely foundational to his philosophical anthropology (Friedman, 2003, p. 57). As a therapist one expects it, as a person, one lives it. One lives it as both I Thou and I It. Distance and relation will be discussed further in Section IV.

Element 4: Healing through Meeting

When the therapist is doing more than general repair work, that is, the client is suffering from an atrophied personal center, then we are bound to approach the client from a relational stance, his or her relations with others, and a deep respect and understanding that the healing takes place from the between. Healing through meeting requires the relational stance, whether it is between the client and their therapist, or client and their family, community, or some mixture of those domains (Friedman, 2003, p.57).

Element 5: The Unconscious Seen as Buber Saw It

In stark contrast to most of the views

about the unconscious prevailing when Buber presented his ideas, the Dialogical Psychotherapist approaches working with the unconscious differently from the way traditional psychology dictates. The unconscious, as Buber viewed it, represents the actual wholeness of the person before the differentiation into psychic and physical, inner and outer, is considered. Freud and Jung made the error that the unconscious was purely psychic. Buber saw his view as a bursting of psychologism and the bursting of this dualism; that is, that such dualisms need not exist between psyche and physical and therefore must not apply to the unconscious. The interesting ramification of this is that it is possible that one unconscious might be in direct communication and meeting with another unconscious (Friedman, 2003, pp.58-59).

Element 6: Existential Guilt

This is not a simple neurotic or inner guilt. It is a guilt that clients will know of deeply, a personal guilt that they have taken on as a person. It can be result from causing an injury of the between, you know that you have it, but you might not know the whereabouts of the person to whom you have committed the offense. Existential guilt might also arise from a violation of shared values or social realities, when one does something in these realms they know they should not have done. There are three steps for fixing this: first, illuminating the guilt (basically admitting it even if you are a different person now); second, persevering even in the face of that illumination (not in self-torture), and if the injury involved others, allowing the light to lead us to a place where we are ready to make reparation; and third (if necessary), repairing the injured order of the world. If the person(s) we have injured is no longer available to us there are numerous places where we can restore the injured order of existence (Friedman, 2003, pp. 60-61).

Element 7: Inclusion or Imagining the Real

This is not the same as empathy (Buber, 1965b), advanced empathy, or identification; it is the full focus on the other, a bold swinging over to the client that makes him fully present to the therapist. At the same time, one does not and must not lose one's own ground. As Friedman says: "If you have been the object of someone's undivided attention, then you have experienced inclusion in genuine dialogue," (2003, p.61). Buber (1965b) describes inclusion as being made up of three elements: first, a relation between two persons, second, an event experienced in common where one actively participates while not sacrificing his or her own reality of the activity, and third, while one, "...at the same time lives through the common event from the standpoint of the other," (p.97).

Element 8: The Problematic of Mutuality

A dialogical psychotherapist (like many therapists) struggles with the degree of mutuality that is present in the therapy, and this mutuality rightfully changes at different stages in the therapy. Still, as Buber (1965a) went to great lengths in his public dialogue with Carl Rogers to point out, Buber's view is that the therapist cannot allow the same demands to be placed upon the client as the client demands of him, so the true nature of therapy must have limited mutuality, or what Buber (1965b) would call one sided inclusion. That is, the therapist must not expect or demand that a full mutuality be present (although it requires some mutuality), as the client is not there to meet the needs of the therapist, but the helping relationship exists for the client. As Friedman puts it: "...it is necessary to recognize that in the healing partnership one person feels a need or lack that leads him or her to come to the other for help and the other is a therapist or counselor who is ready to enter into a relationship to help," (2003, p.63).

Element 9: Confirmation

In spite of other discussions of this concept in this book, confirmation is not a mere act of will on the part of the therapist towards the client. It is based out of the relational stance where the therapist simultaneously experiences both her side of the encounter and the client's. This is the only way we can confirm an other, that is, to see them in their uniqueness. However, this is just part of the process;

the therapist must also be open to what the client brings to the dialogue and the client must also learn existential trust. As Friedman states: "Existential trust of one whole person to another is necessary if the healing of the very roots of the patient's being is to take place," (2003, p.63). Where confirming or accepting the person as they are is a part of this process, it is only the first step. We as therapists must also be concerned with the client's potential, and sometimes we may be called upon by destiny to wrestle with the client to help them embrace it (Friedman 2003, p.63).

Element 10: The Dialogue of Touchstones

Although this represents Friedman's own addition to Dialogical Psychotherapy, he describes them as being made up of both the elements of inclusion and confirmation. Because therapists have greater experience of these elements, they can help the client transcend dualisms and existential traumas like either/or while helping them to remain true to their unique "touchstones of reality," (2003, p. 64). Friedman speculates that if *mental illness* is in part the lack of a shared reality with others, a dialogue of touchstones may help such persons regain a sense of their own personal touchstones of reality through dialogue with others. These persons may need the help of a therapist to do this; a therapist "who can imagine the real and practice inclusion in order to help them enter into a dialogue of touchstones," (2003, p. 65).

Richard Hycner

In Hycner's major work on Dialogical Psychotherapy, he outlines his interpretations of a Dialogical Psychotherapy (Hycner, 1993) that are soundly based on the earlier ideas expounded upon by Buber, Trüb, and Friedman (1985) as well as the Institute of Dialogical Psychotherapy. Therefore, Hycner's interpretation of Dialogical Psychotherapy includes all the prior notions of inclusion, confirmation, the interhuman, and the importance of dialogue, including Friedman's discussion of these and other elements that Friedman includes in the Preface to Hycner's (1993) own book. Hycner then expands upon these ideas, based on both clinical experience and his careful studies of Buber's writings as well as implications drawn from Zen, Gestalt principles, and Transpersonal Psychology. The enduring result is that Hycner makes a valuable new contribution to the formulation of a working approach that enlarges upon Buber and Friedman's earlier works. (Friedman, 1992, noted this regarding Hycner's work).

Along with the above thinkers, Hycner's unique comments are drawn from his personal journey, his clinical practice, and also his enlargement of Hans Trüb's ideas in the dialogical arena of psychotherapy that Buber, Trüb, and Friedman have all termed healing through meeting. As such, Hycner's ideas lay down important foundational additions to our understanding of Dialogical Psychotherapy.

I shall return to a discussion of Trüb's ideas later in this section but here I wish to draw attention to the importance of Hycner's mention of Trüb in helping us understand notions that may often be misunderstood in psychotherapy and counseling. These are the notions of self and other in psychotherapy-or as some have termed it, Dialogical Self and Dialogical Other. Again, from a Buberian perspective, this is merely the confusion of a dialectical aspect or phase of psychotherapy with a truly dialogical one. This is not just a postmodern confusion, for as Friedman (1985) points out, Carl Jung repeatedly stressed that therapy was a process of dialectic that was represented by a dialogue or discussion between two persons.

As both Hycner (1993) and Friedman (1985) note, it was one of Jung's followers who later abandoned Jung's confusion around this notion, and thereby separated dialectic and dialogue into two aspects of a therapeutic approach, namely the psychological-dialectical procedure and the anthropological-dialogical procedure. This dialogical therapist was Hans Trüb.

Hycner (1993) elaborates upon this in his chapter titled: *Dialogical Psychotherapy: Definitions and Overview* where he talks at length about the importance of both aspects of dialectic and dialogue in a Dialogical Psychotherapy. Hycner points out that he is in full agreement with Trüb when he writes that therapy must first be grounded in the dialogical and then move into the intrapsychic or dialectical. (I will note that this seems counter-intuitive from a Western approach, but it should not dismiss this order of work).

Hycner (1993) also dedicates a portion of his work to the spiritual dimension of a Dialogical Psychotherapy. In fact, he goes so far to say that "a dialogical psychotherapy is grounded in a broadly-based spiritual perspective. By no means does it subscribe to any particular religious beliefs, but rather assumes that all human dialogue is grounded in, and is an outgrowth of, a dialogue with Being," (p.78).

William Heard

William Heard is a dialogical therapist who also draws heavily upon the work of Martin Buber to guide his clinical practice. (This reliance upon Buber is one of Friedman's (2003) definitions for being a dialogical psychotherapist). Heard, Friedman, Hycner, and others, have all defined their practice in terms of who they are, their own unique attributes, and have brought new aspects to a Dialogical Psychotherapy.

Among Heard's (1993) unique contributions to Dialogical Psychotherapy is what he termed *Personal Direction*, an addition that Friedman has welcomed as "an important part of Buber's philosophy of dialogue" (Friedman, 2003, p.70). Heard (1993) in his own discussion of personal direction, reminds us that he is not referring to a universal direction for all clients, nor implying that direction comes from the therapist alone (although there is a Buberian notion of wrestling with potential, this refers to the client's potential). Instead personal direction "is only suitable...for the one for whom it is personal," (p.51). Heard (1993) goes on to refer to this as the client's uniqueness, which does not arise from within the client or by introspection but rather arises and unfolds between the client and the therapist. Here there are no predeterminations and preconceptions, "its course remains a mystery until it unfolds in the meeting," (p.51).

Heard (1993) describes seven presuppositions about personal direction that need to be accepted if we are to understand how personal direction works in a Dialogical Psychotherapy. These seven are:

1. Each client possesses a unique multiplicity of possibilities for being.

2. The actualization of these inner possibilities is called out in every encounter with each specific, concrete event in the world throughout the course of the client's lifetime.

3. Such encounters may appear to be randomized givens in the client's existence; however, to the extent that he responds to each concrete event

with his unique, unified personal wholeness, there is meaning and purpose in his life.

4. The client cannot attain the unity of his wholeness within himself. It is found in his interaction with another Thou.

5. It is in ever-renewing dialogue that the client's personal direction emerges, along with his empowerment to pursue it.

6. The client's experience of his personal direction may present him with a knowing that is not always amenable to his rational analysis.

7. To the extent that there is an absence of unity in the client's personal wholeness, there is fragmentation resulting in inner conflict and loss of direction. When this loss occurs, various defenses are brought into play by the disturbed client. At the very core of these defenses is a self-defeating attempt to effect healing without dialogue, (pp.52-53).

Interestingly, Heard's concept of personal direction may help to meet the criticism of Dialogical Psychotherapy that the therapist may inadvertently guide the client into a direction of the therapist's own devising. While this could occur in any form of therapy if the therapist is not careful, the concept of personal direction strongly emphasizes that the direction should come from both client and therapist (with a strong accent on the client). In this respect, Dialogical Psychotherapy is very similar to a Person Centered Approach and not as distinct from it in terms of collaboration as Mouladoudis (2001) seems to depict.

Hans Trüb

Hans Trüb, was a follower of Jung, whom Jung trusted and admired so strongly that he sent his own wife Emma to see the skilled analyst. Trüb, however had a stirring encounter with Buber that shook his world and took him ten years to absorb fully. He later spoke of this encounter as one where he felt he was with another person who really confirmed him as a person, one who had no concern for the characteristics, the training, or the superficialities that Trüb seemed to represent, but truly cared about him as a person. As both Friedman (1985) and Hycner (1993) have pointed out, the work of Trüb has been highly important, with Friedman referring to him as "the fountainhead of dialogical psychotherapy" (Friedman, 1992, p.52).

So, what did Buber have to say about Trüb and the approach of the dialogical psychotherapist? A great deal, it seems. For example, in his Foreword to Trüb's (1952) book, Buber (1952) spoke fondly of Trüb and wrote at length of the paradoxical profession of psychotherapy and the work of the therapist. Similar to things he would later state in his dialogue with Carl Rogers in 1957, this chapter (reprinted in English in Buber, 1952), is very useful in understanding Dialogical Psychotherapy in its own right and deserves careful study.

About Trüb's contributions, Buber (1952) said this: "This way of frightened pause, of unfrightened reflection, of personal involvement, of rejection of security, of unreserved stepping into relationship, of the bursting of psychologism, this way of vision is that which Hans Trüb trod," and, "his foot can no longer push on, but the path is broken. Surely there will not be wanting men like him- awake and daring, hazarding the economics of the vocation, not sparing and not withholding themselves, risking themselves—men who will find his path and extend it further," (both p. 97).

As Friedman (1985) observes, Trüb's approach to psychotherapy was not a mere synthesis of Jung's and Buber's; it was plain that he chose Buber's over Jung's. Friedman notes that if as Buber stated all real living is meeting, and if no healing can take place without meeting (as long as there has been society it has always required an other), then a Dialogical Psychotherapy begins with healing through meeting (the title of Trüb's original book; Friedman, 1992).

Identifying Trüb as a dialogical therapist, Friedman (2003) places both Trüb's procedures (dialectical-psychological and dialogical-anthropological), as Trüb practiced them, soundly within the dialogical approach. And, as he reports, Friedman mentions the important conclusion drawn from Trüb's view, that "the dialectical procedure must be co-ordinated with and subordinated to the dialogical procedure," (1985, p. 30).

The implications of these procedures are, as Friedman (1985) and others have shown us, that the client cannot be understood in terms of mere individual psychology such as feelings, emotions, thoughts (the practice which Buber and others have referred to as *psychologism*), but the whole person must also be understood within the anthropological context from which he or she lives in the world, their culture, and so forth. As such, they must also be understood in terms of the dialogical, that which is between persons, and not just within their head (i.e., dialogue versus dialectic, Friedman, 2003).

As an element of Dialogical Psychotherapy already discussed but enlarged upon here, it should be noted that among Trüb's many contributions was his emphasis of the importance of confirmation in psychotherapy. As Friedman (1992; 2003) has stated, Trüb described two therapy stages. In the first the client presents in a sickened state as a person who has not been confirmed or, worse yet, has been disconfirmed by the world. This has resulted in a withdrawal of the client from authentic dialogue. The client presents as one that needs a confidant, someone to listen to him describe what has happened (or not happened). During that time, the therapist imagines the real, that is, she practices *inclusion* while listening. At the second stage, it is the therapist's task to help the client resume dialogue with the community of which they are a part. To do this, the therapist must sense in part what the demands of the community are. In doing this, Friedman says: "The therapist represents and bears the community values that he or she embodies. Without this second stage — not replacing, but combined with the first stage—there can be no real healing," (2003, p.64).

This concludes Section III where I've discussed some of the basic principles drawn from the work and experience of dialogical psychotherapists that have formed a basic approach to Dialogical Psychotherapy. The interested reader is encouraged to explore these ideas further by consulting the works of these various authors including the works of Buber himself. Bear in mind that this is an approach and not a school of psychotherapy or a group of techniques as Friedman states in the Preface to Hycner's book (1993). It should also be noted that the primary resources mentioned in the Bibliography section of this work are the ultimate authorities in and of themselves concerning Dialogical Psychotherapy. The reader is invited to read them in full. My interpretations are not infallible!

If you think that certain skills are necessary and they seem beyond you, rest assured that they are not the crucial factor. Friedman (1992) states: "What is crucial is not the skill of the therapist, but rather what takes place between the therapist and the client and between the client and other people. The one between cannot totally make up for or take the place of the other," (p.171). What is also important is that a climate of trust has been created and that a client's otherness has been confirmed so that "healing through meeting can flourish on every level," (p.171). My biggest question to you is: Are you ready to face your clients person to person, *from abyss to abyss* and stand with them in *the between*?

SECTION IV. PROBLEMS IN THE PATIENT-THERAPIST CONTEXT

Having just finished Section III, where readers were encouraged not to worry unduly about their skill levels, one should understand this does not mean that a Dialogical Psychotherapy is to be taken lightly, or that no skills are necessary. If you are a trained therapist or counselor then you have some of the skills necessary, but these skills are not what is needed for a Dialogical Psychotherapy to happen. To be open to the context of the unfolding of the between is more than a matter of those skills; it requires an openness to meeting itself, and the dialogue that takes place between you and your client.

In your willingness to approach clients in a

Dialogical Psychotherapy, you may find like any practicing therapist, counselor, or helper, that surprises unfold in the between, that unexpected turns and nooks and crannies appear in your joint dialogue, and yes, that even mismeetings may occur in the healing relationship with a client. This begs the question if a mismeeting can be a part of a healing relationship? Certainly it can, if the mismeeting can be remedied, and if the healing balm is applied. It may take time for the healing balm to work in an injury of the between, it may take considerable effort for existential trust to be re-established, but persistence may be rewarding to both client and therapist.

Clients must learn that challenges and even the aftermath of mismeetings can be worked through and learned from. Life itself is full of mismeetings and sometimes, perhaps many times, it occurs unwittingly or accidentally at the hands of those we love, and yet we go on loving them, and work on restoration and healing. In Dialogical Psychotherapy too, the relationship can recover and the work can continue if the error is not grievous or an ethical violation by the therapist. However, sometimes the injury is too deep or there are other reasons that a therapist and client cannot work together.

So what are some of the common potential problems that occur in the dialogical approach to psychotherapy? Are there any contraindications or groups the therapy should not be applied to? What issues does Dialogical Psychotherapy raise in the relationship between client and therapist? As in any therapy, pitfalls can occur in the unfolding relationship between client and therapist, and since the dialogical approach is primarily one based on relationship, a number of things can be viewed as mishaps- as in other forms of relationships. However, there are some that have been particularly noted in terms of the dialogical.

Some of these issues have already been identified above as actual elements of a Dialogical Psychotherapy but deserve mention again in this context. From its beginning, Dialogical Psychotherapy has been very fair in stating its issues and limitations (for example around inclusion and mutuality). This is probably because its proponents, including Buber himself, were very outspoken and genuine about their experiences from the between. There are always in any approach to another human being some problems that occur more frequently than others, and with some persons that we come to know as clients, particular issues and themes recur because of their own unique histories, our history with them, or simply the unfolding of the between.

Distance and Relation

Already mentioned as underlying the basic going back and forth of the I-Thou and the I-It. The therapist must realize that there will be times in the therapy when he or she perceives a distance and times when the perception is one of nearness in relation. The client cannot stand the constant allness of relation nor can they stand the constant allness of distance. Authentic dialogue demands the going back and forth between the two partners in the healing relationship.

There may be times when there is a sickness in relating, as when the client over relates, or wishes to become over dependent upon the therapist, or perhaps does not seem to want to relate at all. In such cases, our duty is to respond directly so as to remedy this sickness.

The remedies may involve turning towards the other to be available to them and in gentleness engaging them in the dialogical approach (if they decline to relate), and in cases of over dependence it may involve a thickening of the distance. Distance and relation are both essentials in human relations as well as in therapeutic relationships, for, "distance provides the human situation; relation provides man's becoming in that situation," (Buber 1965a, p.64).

The Problematic of Mutuality

Already mentioned as an element of a Dialogical Psychotherapy, Friedman (1985) dedicates an entire chapter to the problem of how much mutuality is possible or desirable in therapeutic encounters. It is essential, Friedman (1985) comments, for the therapist to know when she must lay aside a sense of professional superiority and method to meet the client as a person, so that they are self to self. This is in contrast to knowing that inclusion, (experiencing the other side) is one-sided in psychotherapy (as opposed to friendship and love). That is that the relationship exists for the one needing help.

As Friedman writes in this interesting chapter, where disasters have occurred, when mutuality concerns are ignored, the final outcome of such failure rests primarily with the between. (And perhaps, in my opinion, when unethical actions have occurred by therapists towards their patients, we can see that these are perhaps seen as injuries of the between, that are of course, incidents that therapists may rightfully be held responsible for. Whereas misunderstandings might represent communications or events that could also evolve to the point of a mismeeting, a term which Buber readily understood).

Personal Making Present

Although not necessarily a problem in and of itself but a desired state of attainment, it is one that is a problematic of omission. To work within a dialogical approach requires genuine dialogue. Such dialogue requires that we actually see (or regard) the client for who they really are. In doing so, I accept this person for who they are, affirm them for who they are, confirm them for who they are called to become, even if I must oppose them (I call this the AAC Skill (Kellebrew, 2021). For this to happen requires the mutuality of speech that now arises between us that in turn causes me to legitimize them as a person, one who cares to respond to me in turn. The problematic here is not just to grasp the person but to see them truly in their dynamic center (Buber 1965a).

The Wisdom of Resistance

In Hycner's (1993) book on Dialogical Psychotherapy, he describes a different view of resistance from what is commonly taught. He emphasizes that there is a way to view a client's resistance dialogically; that is, there is a way to turn the resistance around so that the client sees that what he or she is trying to avoid can be creatively tapped into. Although resistance can be viewed as a monologue trying to break out into dialogue, Hycner states that progress can be made. Clients must acknowledge their resistance, appreciate the wisdom of it, and come to realize that there is something invaluable about it.

Other dialogical therapists have identified a number of potential problems in the healing relationship in general, and Dialogical Psychotherapy in particular, and have made suggestions to resolve them. For example, Heard (1993) describes a number of issues in a chapter on the treatment process of a Dialogical Psychotherapy. Among these, he includes case examples that include the *Danger of Fragmentation, Impairments from I-It Relationships,* and, *Danger of Adopting Another's Touchstones* (pp. 148-150).

Therapeutic Considerations Using Dialectic and Dialogue in Patient Groups (Problems with Dualism and Assumptions).

Finally, regarding contraindications, indications, and populations, it should be noted that in most of the literature, dialogical psychotherapists do not differentiate between the application of Dialogical Psychotherapy to different groups based on the severity of psychopathology. In fact, Friedman (1985) talks openly about how the dialogical approach may be helpful to schizophrenics through the benefits of confirmation, as it is the relationship between the client and therapist that they may respond to. (Interestingly, Buck, Buck, Hamm & Lysaker (2016) found this out in their research!)

Similarly, throughout this literature, references are also made to those that suffer from an *atrophied personal center* as being most assisted by Dialogical Psychotherapy. It bears repeating, how Friedman has defined this therapy as a meeting between persons "regardless of whatever therapeutic activities are engaged in" (1992, p. 52; 2003, p.55). Consequently, all clients could benefit from the relationship that is inherent in a dialogical approach.

On the other hand, Smythe (2013) points out that Jung talked about both dialogical aspects and dialectical aspects being present in psychotherapy and that while dialogical work should emphasize work between a person and another person, work that may not be appropriate for someone just wanting to work on basic issues, and that a consensual agreement should be obtained for any in depth work that could be considered more dialogical. (Which is echoed in a distinction that is often made between counseling and psychotherapy as well). But here I am really diluting the issue, as Smythe (2013) is not necessarily talking about a Dialogical Psychotherapy from the same perspective as Friedman and followers. (It is interesting to note the similarity however). The latter notion of a Dialogical Psychotherapy arose from Buber's dialogical stance, which for dialogical therapists means working with a patient person to person while respecting and allowing those experiences of healing through meeting to happen, no matter what one's therapeutic orientation is being ascribed to.

This is not to say that further research will not identify groups that are especially suited or more suited to a dialectical or a dialogical approach. From the perspective of dialectic, there are already established research examples of possible differences between patient groups. And it may very well be that the dialectical procedure that Trüb and others noted, (the intrapsychic dialectical procedure mentioned earlier) would be especially helpful to certain kinds of patients who are more able to do such work and make a commitment to do such.

In light of such differences, there may be some nuggets of truth after all. For example: dialectical thinking skills, could be even more suited for those who have reached a post-formal stage of cognitive development, as the early research supposed (Basseches, 1984), or for those who show the ability to engage in such thinking skills. For example, the ability to tolerate ambiguity (a hallmark of dialectical thinking) or to understand that between two opposing views there might be a middle ground (Linehan, 1993).

And yet another example from the dialectical frame of reference would be the work of Marsha Linehan (1993) and Dialectical Behavior Therapy (DBT). DBT research shows that people can receive great benefit from a dialectical approach that is skills based. That is, by teaching them skills that they can use again and again to help them build a life worth living (Linehan 2020). Among them are DBT skills based on Mindfulness, Emotion Regulation, Distress Tolerance, and Interpersonal Effectiveness (Linehan, 1993). These skills, originally developed (with strong evidence based support) for Borderline Personality Disorder and highly suicidal patients, have now been shown to be helpful to both adults and adolescents and is widely taught in all sorts of inpatient and outpatient group settings with all kinds of people. Of these, the core aspect of Mindfulness and Wise Mind has been widely talked about, as there are various forms of Mindfulness training that are quite popular in therapy circles at this time.

While mentioning that there are approaches that are openly based on dialectical concepts, it is helpful and interesting to note that dialogical work may have levels of similarity to dialectical work, while also remembering that the dialogical is quite different. (A chance to practice your dialectical thinking here). Regardless, it is easy to hypothesize that those who work well with dialectics could bring an openness that could be quite beneficial in a Dialogical Psychotherapy.

Similarly, some of the developmental differences or blocks in different patient groups might also be present in both levels of work. Although easy to hypothesize, one would not want to overstate any sort of developmental level to the level of bias, as there may be other factors, such as good old motivation to get better. After all, as Linehan has often said, when we find that we are stuck or continue to suffer, it may only be a matter of finding out what skill we can use to get out of it. The alternative of not choosing to use any skill, is to continue to suffer.

This idea of a developmental prerequisite or attainment before doing dialectical or dialogical work is an interesting idea that may be dated, however. There are other aspects to development beside neo-Piagetian ones. Although Linehan does cite Basseches (1984) in some early papers (Heard & Linehan, 1994), DBT has certainly evolved to help many kinds of people.

It might be an interesting research project to see if people of a certain chronological age or level of cognitive development have better outcomes while doing dialectical work or a Dialogical Psychotherapy, but one thing is clear, many people can be helped no matter what developmental level they are at, if they are met person to person, and together, they find a personal way to use what they are being taught

In summary, while the early research in dialectical reasoning often assumed a college level sample was necessary, that doesn't mean that this was the only group that could benefit. Perhaps the teaching of dialectical skills advances development across all age groups, with different levels of understanding and engagement that are not linked to an assumed chronological age or stage theory of cognitive development, but rather a willingness to implement and use the skills effectively.

Teaching for empowerment seems more accurate than assuming there may be limitations! Surely the teaching materials used may reflect adult and adolescent differences or child levels of understanding, but the principles of dialectical thinking and the ability to tolerate opposing points of view seems well established in patients of varying ages and even diagnoses. DBT may be clearly indicated and empirically shown to be helpful to those suffering from Borderline Personality Disorder, but there are many skills in DBT that can help almost anyone!

Still, I do think there is something to be said about thinking outside any box while doing therapy, that simply requires an openness in any therapy to what is happening between you and the patient. And any such openness to helping as we approach any client or patient; ought to be one where we meet them, to help them with the full attention they deserve as one who is asking for help and as we therapists are the ones called alongside to help.

I do think that any presupposed distinctions within any approach (even dialogical and dialectical ones) are as artificial as to any endeavor, as one can relate with a client at whatever level they are at and many skills can still be taught to people beginning with where they are at. One is there for them and with them. And a dialogical therapist can no doubt experience life changing moments of meeting with people of many ages, backgrounds, and worldviews. Perhaps one empowering outcome of a dialogical therapy is to appreciate the differences of others and how a certain kind of knowing can be beneficial to all.

In the final analysis, while there are skills and techniques appropriate to certain issues, groups, or even situations, and to not do what one should as a therapist would be malpractice, or behaving in certain unhelpful ways could lead to mismeetings, any true dialogical moment does not happen by being trained for it, because ultimately, the I-Thou moments of healing through meeting, happen simply by grace. These are the significant moments of meeting, which as Buber (1958) says, all real living is meeting.

SECTION V.
CONCLUSION

In this brief work, I have introduced readers to a brief history, overview, and the common pitfalls of a Dialogical Psychotherapy based upon Martin Buber's philosophy of the interhuman as it has been applied to the healing relationship. Basic elements have been identified and texts have been listed that can offer more information to interested readers and therapists.

Because of Buber's experience as a mystic himself, and the seemingly mystical components of his dialogical approach (e.g., the term *inclusion* originates from Hasidic roots, Friedman, 1992); some readers might misconstrue Dialogical Psychotherapy as overly religious or spiritual, and find this to be a roadblock for them. Others, because of its ontological claims, and the inability to adequately measure the interhuman realm (or the between), might criticize Dialogical Psychotherapy as *non-scientific* or too steeped in experiential terms to be acceptable. Lest the previous sentence offend anyone (let alone dialogical therapists), let me point out that Hycner (1993) has reported that the distinction between nomothetic knowledge and idiographic knowledge has been bridged in his consciousness as someone practicing as a dialogical therapist and is useful for anyone contemplating it. One must have enough scientific knowledge to approach a therapeutic relationship generally (that is the concept of training that I referred to earlier). Such is the nomothetic knowledge. And one must also allow the uniqueness of the situation to unfold in the therapy that is before one, and such is the idiographic distinction of knowledge.

In general, the dialogical theory of knowledge differs from other forms of knowledge that are based more upon I-It. As Friedman (1965) signifies, it is easy to criticize Buber's philosophical anthropology for its apparent lack of objectivity concerning authenticity, but this is to come at it from the study of persons as objects, in short, it is to confuse the issue by not seeing Buber's dialogical theory of knowledge.

What should be understood clearly, is that Buber's philosophical anthropology is not meant to do away with or replace the sciences or empirical disciplines that study human persons as objects, but rather to find another perspective within it; namely, how it is that the person becomes a Thou.

Finally, Friedman points out that there is a difference between the approach of the psychologist and the anthropologist. The psychologist seeks to find out by observing and remaining outside of what is happening, but the anthropologist is considerably more like a participant observer, or one that looks at the essentials. (I do think that there are many psychologists who could identify with both perspectives!)

If they allow themselves to be repelled by such features as the lack of scientism, or the fact that it seems *too spiritual* or religious, potential dialogical psychotherapists prevent themselves from learning about a psychotherapy that is solidly based on the relationship and what happens between two persons engaged in a dialogue between one who is hurting and one who is called alongside to help. One must see the possibility that there can be a dialogical encounter between person and person, and that both persons can enter into a Dialogical Psychotherapy. If we can do so, then we can start to move into a very interesting framework around the old problems of subject and object and self and other that have plagued systems of thought for centuries. To grasp this we must be able to move eventually from non-Buberian notions of a *dialogical self* to something else entirely, and we must view the concept of the unconscious differently (as Buber saw it) if we are to move ahead in new directions of understanding how a Dialogical Psychotherapy can become even more powerfully utilized in the healing relationship between person and person.

Although both dialectic and dialogue are aspects of a Dialogical Psychotherapy,(already shown from the work of Trüb (1952) and Hycner (1993)), one of the best hopes for resolving the notion of a dualistic relation of dialectic and dialogue would be understanding them as a developmental process. Interestingly, this may also help Dialogical Psychotherapy to begin to address something that Heard (1993) pointed out was still a frontier in the realm of the dialogical approach at the time he wrote his book, namely how the dialogical plays a role in human development, and how Dialogical Psychotherapy may be, in part, a developmental therapy. (Basseches and Mascolo (2010), would likely agree, pointing out that psychotherapy by its very nature, is developmental).

Indeed the spirit of Heard's (1993) inquiry seems to give greater emphasis to development than what has been typically given in terms of a dialogical psychotherapy; namely in remarking that there is no I without a Thou (a notion which goes back before Buber to Jacobi, Dilthey, and Feuerbach) and in discussions about how Object Relations Theory is similar to the interplay of I-Thou and I-It.

Since a good dialogical work does not therefore reject dialectical work, it goes back and forth from it to its dialogical foundation. It would do us well to understand that splitting dialectical and dialogical work behooves us to remember that dichotomous explanations may artificially split unities into functional dualisms that are transcended when we are considering/seeking seed of truth representations. We may be able to see that we begin from one place and progress to another when we move from dialectic to dialogue or vice versa. For if our perspective of dialectic were simply seen as intrapsychic and dialogue as esteeming the other point of view—we may have useful understandings, but we must observe and allow the exchange of the two to historically play out in our own moments of development and the development of any of our patients that we are doing dialogical work with.

On the other hand, it would seem from the works of Hycner (1991; 1993), Trüb (1952), and in the mention of Trüb by Friedman (1985) that dialectic may be understood as a monological, intrapsychic event that sometimes attains the level of genuine dialogue as it unfolds in the between of the healing relationship.

As Trüb (1952) has pointed out, both a dialectical-psychology procedure and a dialogical-anthropological procedure takes place in healing through meeting. Later, Hycner (1993) was to refer to these procedures as *"the dialectical-intrapsychic, and, the dialogical-interpersonal,"* respectively (p.90). When considering any procedure in doing therapy work, we often wonder (both patients and therapists) as to how long it will take? This is a highly personal question, although psychotherapy outcome studies often have a definite number of treatment sessions, such research is looking for positive clinical outcomes such as symptomatic reduction or relief. Which is of course the most important outcome we are looking for as therapists.

When doing dialectical work however, the notion of dialectic begs a question about the passage of time; i.e., how long does it take for a dialectic to resolve? In philosophical terms it seems, there is no set interval, as we are talking about relational events that represent crisis points that are followed by resolutions. Perhaps the resolution of the dialectic occurs after the therapy hour in the person's real-life settings? Perhaps revolutions do not necessarily come in the public moments, but when one is privately examining the evidence or meeting the problems of everyday life. (Perhaps with some new skills they just learned). Similarly, even in the growth of science, we have the movement through anomalies to a crisis point, and a corresponding resolution where a paradigm shift may be said to have occurred, resulting in a revolution or new worldview (Kuhn, 1970).

The relation between the person and their thinking apparatus and the relation of the therapist with the patient and the communication (genuine dialogue) that ensues are two factors crucial to any developmental therapy. In the dialogical perspective, the relationship between therapist and patient may provide opportunities for the deliberate induction of a dialectical view through dialogue, or at least, aids in the resolution of a dialectical conflict into a moment of development through genuine dialogue. But that is not the purpose of a Dialogical Psychotherapy, for there is another element that is just as crucial as requiring another person, that is, that dialogical therapists practice healing through meeting as a central component to any dialogical therapy (Friedman, 1985; Friedman in Hycner, 1991). And of course, there is this phenomenological event, that although it seems hoped for, it at times most certainly unfolds; and that is the moment of meeting; which according to Buber is an I-Thou moment of grace.

As we know, at various times, applications from psychology and psychotherapy can spread to other domains of knowledge. Dialogue can resolve conflicts at the international and societal levels (Kellebrew, 2013), but the emphasis on outcomes are different.

In terms of psychology, findings from the dialogical may become features of developmental psychology in the sense that Heard (1993) has hinted at.

Similarly, a broad research base has postulated that there is a level of development involving dialectical reasoning or dialectical thinking which represents a stage beyond formal reasoning in the Piagetian schemata of development (Basseches,

1984). This would seem to place dialectical work in the developmental scheme of things.

Later, Basseches and Mascolo (2010) indicated that Basseches' earlier work on dialectical thinking for adults might be expanded into viewing psychotherapy as part of an overall developmental process. The results of both of these movements is a fulfillment of Trüb's (1952) pioneering vision, with his notion of the two procedures, i.e., dialectic (internal) and dialogue (external) manifestations of mind.

One is led to wonder if it is possible that dialogue from a Buberian perspective will develop into as much of a developmental therapy model as dialectic has been developed into a therapeutic model? (Some would say the latter is already well represented with Linehan's DBT (1993). Equally, some would say that a Dialogical Psychotherapy has already been well pioneered or well formulated by the dialogical therapists and the works mentioned in this book.

In his discussion of the history of the dialogical principle, Buber (1965b) discusses influences on the development of his philosophy. It is interesting that his ideas were emerging at the same time as the Freudian and Jungian schools, with their emphasis on the unconscious. These were not major influences, as Buber was primarily influenced by his teacher Dilthey and others. And, as noted above, he developed his own view on the unconscious, one which was quite different from anyone else's at the time. It is a view that allows for inclusion, confirmation, and other concepts inherent in a Dialogical Psychotherapy that work in the between.

Buber's view was so different in the way it viewed the unconscious as a whole, before it is split into psychic and physical; and did not see it as a merely psychic event. It has to do with the whole person and therefore makes it possible for the whole person to connect with others in ways that other models do not allow. It is a view of the unconscious that transcends dualism and the problem of other minds and their own unconscious. It is quite possible in a Buberian approach for one unconscious to communicate to another. Imagine how understanding this more fully might impact the healing relationship!

In conclusion, we have seen that Buber's dialogical philosophy makes powerful contributions to a Dialogical Psychotherapy that makes contact with others in a special ontological sphere of relation called the between. During the process of such a therapy a genuine dialogue is achieved, followed by acceptance, affirmation, and confirmation, and perhaps unfolding of the client's potential to become someone different.

The person is affirmed in the meeting with the therapist who boldly swings into their very lives while keeping one foot solidly resting in their own world as well. Through such acts of inclusion, the therapist receives a special sense of the work necessary in the therapeutic relationship.

During the therapy special problems may come up like the problematic of mutuality, existential guilt, and resistance; the dialogical therapist, who is sensitive to the issues unfolding in the between is able to respond to the client's need.

These responses are the dialogical therapy itself, that is, the relationship and the between, as there are no inherent techniques that can capture the between, they can only be used in the now and in the making present of the client in a true dialogical approach.

In the dialogical approach as outlined here there are no rapidly acquired skills and techniques that can teach one to be a dialogical therapist. One builds upon one's already existent skills and training as a therapist, or counselor, approaching a client with the willingness to relate.

Likewise, the approach of a Dialogical Therapy is best thought of as captured in a relational event, as it is not mere communication or speech acts but rather an experience of encounter. One simply lives the dialogical.

Ultimately, if there were skills, they would include the skill and focus of a trained healer turning to another in full attention. In this relation and mindfulness of dialogical themes, one prepares for the hopeful relational event of the graceful appearing of an I-Thou. This is the approach between person and person that culminates in healing through meeting.

BIBLIOGRAPHY

Bakhtin, M. M. (1986) *Speech Genres and Other Late Essays.* Trans. by Vern W. McGee. Austin, TX: University of Texas Press.

Basseches, M. (1984) *Dialectical Thinking and Adult Development.* Norword, NJ: Ablex Books.

Basseches, M. & Mascolo, M. F. (2010) *Psychotherapy as a Developmental Process.* New York: Routledge/Taylor & Francis Group, LLC.

Buber, M. (1952) *Pointing the Way.* Trans. and Ed. By Maurice Friedman. New York: Schocken Books.

Buber, M. (1958) *I and Thou.* 2nd rev. ed. Trans. Ronald Gregor Smith. New York: Charles Scribner's Sons.

Buber, M. (1965a) *The Knowledge of Man: A Philosophy of the Interhuman.* Trans. Maurice S. Friedman and Ronald G. Smith. Edited by Maurice Friedman. New York: Harper & Row.

Buber, M. (1965b) *Between Man and Man.* M. Friedman (Ed). New York: Collier Books.

Buber, M. (1999) *Martin Buber on Psychology and Psychotherapy: Essays, Letters, and Dialogue.* J. Agassi-Buber (Ed). Syracuse, NY: Syracuse University Press

Buck, K. D., Buck, B. E., Hamm, J. A. & Lysaker, P. H. (2016) Martin Buber and evidence-based practice: Can the lion really lie down with the lamb?, *Psychosis*, 8:2, 156-165.

Friedman, M. (1965) Introductory Essay. in: M. Friedman and R.G. Smith. (Trs.) and M. Friedman (Ed.) *The Knowledge of Man: A Philosophy of the Interhuman.* New York: Harper and Row.

Friedman, M. (1975) Healing through meeting: A dialogical approach to psychotherapy, *American Journal of Psychoanalysis*, 35, (3 & 4).

Friedman, M. (1976) *Martin Buber: The Life of Dialogue.* 3rd Ed. Revised. Chicago: University of Chicago Press.

Friedman, M. (1981) *Martin Buber's Life and Work: The Early Years, 1878-1923.* New York: E.P. Dutton.

Friedman, M. (1985) *The Healing Dialogue in Psychotherapy.* New York: Jason Aronson.

Friedman, M. (1986) *Martin Buber and the Eternal.* New York: Human Sciences Press.

Friedman, M. (1989) Personal communication with the author.

Friedman, M. (1992) *Religion and Psychology: A Dialogical Approach*. New York: Paragon House Publishers.

Friedman, M. (2003) Martin Buber and Dialogical Psychotherapy, in: R. Frie (Ed.) *Understanding Experience: Psychotherapy and Postmodernism.* New York: Routledge.

Friedman, M. (2008) Buber and Dialogical Therapy: Healing Through Meeting, *The Humanistic Psychologist,* 36:3-4, 298-315.

Heard, W. G. (1993) *The Healing Between: A Clinical Guide to Dialogical Psychotherapy.* Foreword by Maurice Friedman. San Francisco, CA: Jossey Bass.

Heard, H. L. & Linehan, M. M. (1994) Dialectical Behavior Therapy: An Integrative Approach to the Treatment of Borderline Personality Disorder. *Journal of Psychotherapy Integration,* 4, 55-82.

Hermans, H. J. M. (2002) The Dialogical Self as a Society of Mind: Introduction. *Theory and Psychology* 12(2), 147-160.

Hycner, R. H. (1991) *Between Person and Person: Toward a Dialogical Psychotherapy.* Preface by Maurice Friedman. Highland, NY: The Center for Gestalt Development, Inc.

Hycner, R. H. (1993) *Between Person and Person: Toward a Dialogical Psychotherapy.* Preface by Maurice Friedman. Highland, NY: The Gestalt Journal Press.

Kellebrew, T. (1984) *Subject-Object Deliberation and the Mechanics of True Communication* (unpublished paper).

Kellebrew, T. (1988) *Dialectical Thinking and Its Implications for Psychotherapy* (unpublished paper).

Kellebrew, T. (1998) *Dialectical Thinking and Dialogical Relating: Their Implications for Development* (unpublished MA project).

Kellebrew, T. (2006) Dialogical Self, Dialogical Other: A Brief Overview of Dialogical Psychotherapy. *Practical Philosophy*, 17-27.

Kellebrew, T. (2012) *Brief Overview of Dialogical Psychotherapy,* First Edition. Portland, OR: TiLu Press, LLC.

Kellebrew, T. (2013) *On the World as Misrepresentation.* Portland, OR: TiLu Press

Kellebrew, T. (2021) *Dialectic and Dialogue in Psychotherapy and Counseling.* (To be published by TiLu Press, LLC).

Kron, T. & Friedman, M. (1994) Problems of Confirmation in Psychotherapy. *Journal of Humanistic Psychology*; 34(1), 66-83.

Kuhn, T. (1970) *The Structure of Scientific Revolutions.* 2nd Ed. Chicago, IL: University of Chicago Press.

Leiman, M. (2004) Dialogical Sequence Analysis. In H. H. Hermans & G. Dimaggio, (Eds.), *The Dialogical Self in Psychotherapy.* New York: Routledge.

Linehan, M. M. (1993) *The Skills Training Manual for Treating Borderline Personality Disorder.* New York: Guilford.

Linehan, M. M. (2020) *Building a Life Worth Living: A Memoir.* New York: Penguin Random House.

Mouladoudis, G. (2001) Dialogical and Person-Centered Approach to Psychotherapy: Beyond Correspondences and Contrasts, Toward a Fertile Interconnection, *The Person-Centered Journal,* 8(1), 4-15.

Smythe, W.E. (2013) The Dialogical Jung: Otherness within the Self, *Behavioral Scientist* (Basel) Nov. 21;3(4), 634-646.

Trüb, H. (1952) *Heilung aus der Beregnung. Eine Aueinandersetzung mit der Psychologie .* C. G. Jung. by Ernst Michel and Arie Sborowitz (Eds.), Stuttgart: Ernst Klett Verlag.

ABOUT THE AUTHOR

Tim L. Kellebrew

Tim Kellebrew is a mental health therapist with over 36 years of experience working in outpatient and inpatient settings doing individual therapy, case management, group therapy, and supervision. He currently resides in Portland, Oregon where he conducts group therapy and works as a consultant and educator. He has done graduate work at a number of universities and professional schools including the Institute of Dialogical Psychotherapy. He also works as a businessman and entrepreneur in various fields, including healthcare, emerging technologies (such as AI), and content marketing. In his spare time, he pursues his interests in reading, film, and writing, where in addition to publications under his own name, he has been published with pseudonyms in poetry, nonfiction, and fiction.